West China
Panorama

First Edition 2002

West China Panorama

ISBN 7-119-03116-3

© Foreign Languages Press
Published by Foreign Languages Press
24 Baiwanzhuang Road, Beijing 100037, China
Home Page: http://www.flp.com.cn
E-mail Addresses: info@flp.com.cn
sales@flp.com.cn
Distributed by China International Book Trading Corporation
35 Chegongzhuang Xilu, Beijing 100044, China
P.O. Box 399, Beijing, China

Printed in the People's Republic of China

West China Panorama

By Huang Wei

Foreign Languages Press   Beijing

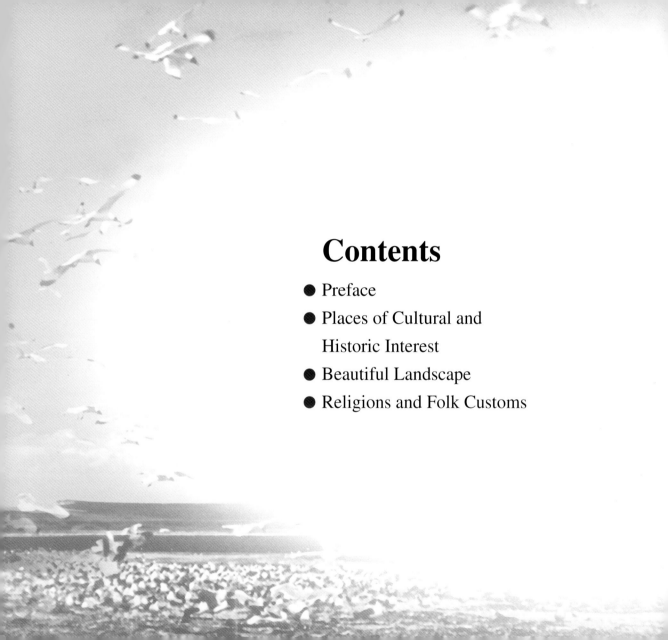

Contents

- Preface
- Places of Cultural and Historic Interest
- Beautiful Landscape
- Religions and Folk Customs

Preface

Situated in the central part of the Asian continent, the western region of China is on the rooftop of the world. With an area larger than half of Europe, it has a favorable geographical location. From west China, one can easily travel westward to reach Central Asian countries and even Amsterdam in Europe. It adjoins Southeast Asia and the South Asian subcontinent in the southwest, and the Beibu Gulf and South China Sea in the south. The region encompasses one-third of China s administrative regions—Shaanxi, Gansu, Qinghai, Sichuan, Yunnan and Guizhou provinces, Chongqing Municipality, and the Ningxia Hui, Xinjiang Uygur, Guangxi Zhuang, Inner Mongolia and Tibet autonomous regions. Covering 5.4 million square km, west China equals 56 percent of the nation s total land area, and supports a population of 280 million, or 23 percent of the national total.

To get to know west China, begin with its most famous waterways, the Yangtze and Yellow rivers, both of which have nurtured the country s 5,000-year-old civilization. Taking melted glacial and snow water from the Kunlun and Himalayan mountains in the western region, the Yangtze and Yellow rivers flow eastward before emptying into the sea.

The western region has abundant natural resources. Alongside its rich water resources, which account for 82.5 percent of the national total, it also has considerable mineral deposits. Statistics provided by the Ministry of Land and Resources show that the northwestern region has great potential for development of mineral resources, with the potential value of their reserves estimated at 33.7 trillion yuan. The western region boasts of having over 120 of the 150 types of minerals discovered in China so far, including coal, petroleum, natural gas, nickel, copper, lead, zinc, gold and potash salt. The recoverable reserves of the region s coal, which constitute 30 percent of the national total, are mainly distributed in Shaanxi, Xinjiang and Ningxia. The region holds 510 million tons, or nearly 23 percent, of the country s total underground oil reserves, which are chiefly deposited in the Ordos Basin, Junggar Basin, Tarim Basin, Turpan-Kumul Basin and Qaidam Basin. Its natural gas reserves, distributed in the Ordos and Tarim basins, stand at 135.4 billion cubic meters, 58 percent of the national total. In addition, 62 percent of the country s total nickel reserves and 57 percent of its platinum reserves are concentrated in the western province of Gansu, and 97 percent of potash salt reserves are in Qinghai Province. Both nationally and internationally, the region also ranks first in terms of reserves of some rare metals.

The two major national projects under construction—the west-to-east gas transmission and west-to-east power transmission—well demonstrate the role of the western region in national economic development. To tap abundant natural gas resources in the west, the Chinese Government invested in building a 4,000-km pipeline. Stretching across nine provinces, autonomous regions and municipalities, the pipeline will transmit gas from the west to the eastern region, which will not only ease the energy shortage in east China but also help reduce environmental pollution there. The western region has sufficient waterpower resources, and power transmission facilities have been constructed or are being built, which will transmit electricity to power deficient cities in the east.

However, what makes the western region so attractive is its beautiful landscape, abundant sites of cultural and historic interest, unique religious rituals and colorful folklore. As many places in the west remain undeveloped, its natural environment is free of pollution and local cultural traditions retain their primitive and simple forms. Therefore, the region is an ideal place to review history, find traditions and enjoy the primitive charms of nature.

West China is one of the world s regions boasting the richest tourist resources. Many of its scenic spots have been included in the World Cultural Heritage List, the World Natural Heritage List or the World Cultural and Natural Heritage List. Forty-five sites have been listed as national- or provincial-level scenic spots or places of interest, and 72 areas have been included among nature reserves and environment conservation zones designated by the State or international organizations.

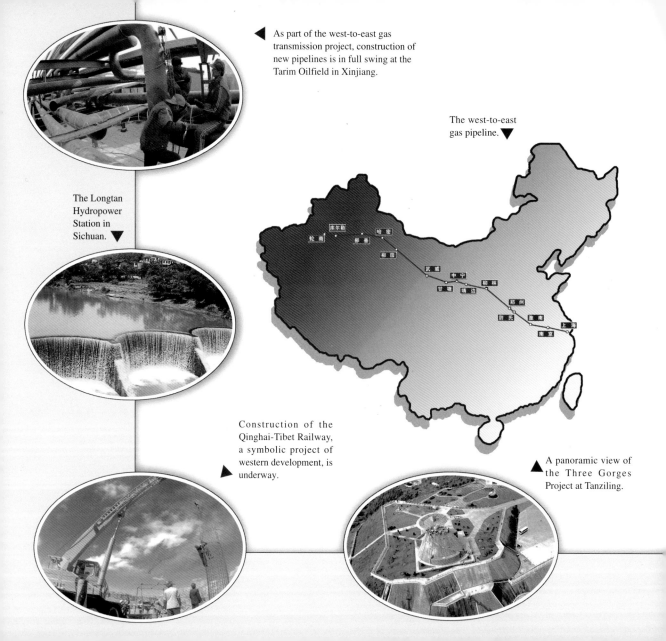

As part of the west-to-east gas transmission project, construction of new pipelines is in full swing at the Tarim Oilfield in Xinjiang.

The west-to-east gas pipeline. ▼

The Longtan Hydropower Station in Sichuan. ▼

Construction of the Qinghai-Tibet Railway, a symbolic project of western development, is underway.

A panoramic view of the Three Gorges Project at Tanziling.

库尔勒
轮南   哈密
    库车
        柳园
            武威
            中宁   柳林
        甘塘 靖边
                郑州
            尉氏 淮南
                    上海
                南京

The map of the Qinghai-Tibet Railway.

The sketch map of the west-to-east electric power transmission project. ▶

A street market in Kangding county seat.▼

A bird's-eye view of Urumqi, Xinjiang.◤

SACRED
Revolutionary Places

Site of the Zunyi Meeting

Cemetery of Red Army Revolutionary Martyrs at Xiaolong Mountain, Zunyi.

A sculpture in front of the Red Army Martyrs Tomb in Zunyi.

Among the myriads of sites of historic interest, the cities of Yan an and Zunyi have captured great attention. Yan an in Shaanxi Province and Zunyi in Guizhou Province were two shining stars during the decades of Chinese revolution led by the Communist Party of China (CPC). The CPC Central Committee held an enlarged meeting of the Political Bureau in Zunyi on January 15-17, 1935, which determined the leadership of Mao Zedong in the Red Army and the CPC. This meeting marked an important turning point in the history of the CPC. Zunyi hence became one of the sacred places of revolution revered by the people. Yan an became the revolutionary base and center of Chinese revolution after the arrival of the Red Army in October 1935, where the CPC led the Chinese people to win the War of Resistance Against Japanese Aggression and shatter the Kuomintang s machination of civil war. The Chinese revolution achieved final victory in 1949 with the founding of the People s Republic of China.

The former residence of Mao Zedong in Yan'an.

The Central Auditorium at Yangjialing, Yan'an, where the Seventh National Congress of the CPC was held in 1945.

Yan'an City today, with the Tower Hill in the distance.

Places of Cultural and Historic Interest

Historical ruins of human civilization found in west China can be traced back to the prehistoric period. Some 2 million years ago, Wushan Man, living in the drainage area of the Daning River, had already made tools, distinguishing themselves from animals, which rely solely on nature. Yuanmou Man illuminated the course of human civilization with their torchlight 1.7 million years ago. Lantian Man created the new stone axe age 1 million years ago, while in Xi'an, beautiful designs appeared on earthenware made by Banpo Man 6,000 years ago. The 5,000-year-old designs of dances were found on the pottery fragments excavated in Qinghai, and relics of the Neolithic Age at the maximum height above sea level were unearthed in the Qomolangma Nature Reserve.

West China also boasts numerous cultural relics and historic sites over the last 5,000 years, including the Qinshihuang Mausoleum, Dunhuang Grottoes, Potala Palace, Great Buddha Statue at Leshan and Dazu Stone Sculptures. Many of them have been included in the World Cultural Heritage List and the World Cultural and Natural Heritage List.

Primeval Historic Sites

Shaanxi has been considered the cradle of Chinese civilization, because of its location of strategic importance in ancient China, which linked the northwestern and southwestern parts with the Central Plains. Over 30,000 cultural relics and historic sites were found here. Among them are the Lantian Culture and Dali Culture of the Paleolithic Age and the Neolithic Yangshao Culture at the Banpo Site. Situated on the eastern outskirts of Xi'an, the Banpo Site presents the scene of the matrilineal commune in the drainage area of the Yellow River 6,000 years ago. Ruins of their living quarters, pottery workshops and clan graves provide a profile of their quotidian life and funerals. Nearly 10,000 pieces of production tools and utensils have been unearthed here. The mat and textile impressions, geometric patterns, designs of animals and plants, and engraved simple symbols on the pottery ware give later generations clues of their mentality.

The Yunnan-Guizhou Plateau cannot be counted out of the birthplace of primitive humans. It was in Yunnan that archeologists found traces of Yuanmou Man living 1.7 million years ago, which provides

A bronze galloping horse of the Eastern Han Dynasty (25-220), unearthed in Wuwei County, Gansu.

Prehistoric painted earthenware unearthed in Gansu.

An Eastern Han stone carving of plowing with oxen, unearthed in Mizhi County, Shaanxi.

The Famen Temple in Shaanxi.

Painted bronze horses and chariot.

Qin Terracotta Warriors and Horses.

strong evidence for the hypothesis that humans also evolved from Asia. Geographical and environment changes during the long geological eras left Guizhou 50 Pre-Paleolithic sites, over 20 of which have been excavated, yielding tens of thousands of human fossils and other cultural relics.

Gansu has always captured the attention of archeologists at home and abroad. Numerous primitive culture sites have been found here, including the Neolithic Majiayao Culture dating back to over 4,000 years. The Majiayao painted pottery marked not only the highest level of Chinese painted pottery culture, but also represented the world's most brilliant achievements in this regard in ancient times.

Many rarely visited places in the western region have proved to be the paradise of humans in remote antiquity. For instance, the Pre-Paleolithic ruins, discovered along the Tuotuo River on the Qinghai-Tibet Plateau and in Hoh Xil and Qaidam Basin, indicate that human activities took place here about 30,000 years ago. Archeological studies demonstrate that 30,000 years ago, primitive people in Ningxia lived on rhinoceros, wild asses, water buffalo and ostrich. Yarlung Zangbo Grand Canyon also contains traces of primitive humans living 8,000 years ago.

The Silk Road

Connecting Asia with Europe, the Silk Road has a history of more than 2,000 years as the most famous overland trade route in ancient times. The 7,000-km-long route started from Chang'an (present-day Xi'an) in the east, stretched for over 4,000 km in China passing through Shaanxi, Gansu, Ningxia, Qinghai and Xinjiang, and then crossed over the Pamirs before reaching the eastern coast of the Mediterranean Sea via Central Asia. Through this route, China's unique techniques, such as sericulture, porcelain, the use of the compass, paper making, the art of printing and the manufacture of gunpowder, entered the West, while Western religions, music, acrobatics, and plant and grain crop seeds were brought into China.

Today, the numerous cultural relics, historic sites, imposing natural scenery and colorful folklore of various ethnic groups along the ancient Silk Road have attracted tens of thousands of tourists from across the world. Historic and cultural sites that remain to greet tourists include the Qin Terracotta Warriors and Horses, and Famen Temple where bones of Sakyamuni are enshrined, the Mogao Grottoes, the Jiayuguan Pass of the Great Wall, Tar Monastery of Tibetan Buddhism, and the Ruins of the Ancient City of Gaochang.

A bronze *hu*, wine vessel, of the Western Zhou Dynasty (c.11th century-771 BC), unearthed in Fufeng County, Shaanxi. ▼

Great Wild Goose Pagoda in Xi'an, Shaanxi.

A corner of the ancient city wall of Xi'an.

The Qamba Buddha Statue at Tashilhungpo
Monastery in Xigaze, Tibet.

The Holy Stupa for the remains of the 10th Panchen
Lama enshrined in Tashilhungpo Monastery, Tibet.

The Potala Palace in Lhasa, Tibet Autonomous Region.

Ruins of the Guge Kingdom in Tibet.

Natural attractions include the Bird Island of Qinghai Lake, the Flaming Mountain in Turpan, the Swan Nature Reserve in Bayanbulak Grassland, the Tianchi Lake in Tianshan Mountain and the Salt Lake in Qinghai. Furthermore, the Silk Road traverses areas where ethnic minorities live in compact communities. These hospitable minority ethnic groups, who are talented in singing and dancing, attract tourists with their distinct customs, unique cultures and religious beliefs.

Jiayuguan Pass

Situated to the southwest of Jiayuguan City, Gansu, the Jiayuguan Pass was so named as it was built at the foot of Jiayu Mountain. Constructed in 1372, it was the western terminus of the Great Wall of the Ming Dynasty (1368-1644). Walls of Jiayuguan Fort, which covers 33,500 square meters, are 733 meters long and 11.7 meters high. The four corner towers, two stories high, appear like fortresses. Standing on the tower, you get a sweeping view of the northern-frontier scene.

Grotto Art

Ever since its introduction into China from India, along with Buddhism, in the fifth century, grotto art had developed steadily in China till its heyday in the Sui and Tang (618-907) dynasties, leaving huge numbers of precious grottoes in China, mostly in the western part.

The Mogao Grottoes in Dunhuang Situated 25 km to the southeast of Dunhuang County, Gansu, the Mogao Grottoes, carved out of rocks in a stretch of 1.6 km along the eastern side of Mingshashan or Singing Sand Dune, are the largest and most famous Buddhist grottoes in China. First built in 366, the grottoes are known as the Thousand-Buddha Caves. Covering 45,000 square meters, murals in the remaining 492 grottoes depict the diverse social culture of different times. Weathering hundreds of years of wind and sand, they are still bright in color and clear in lines. There are also over 2,100 painted sculptures of different sizes. Traditional Indian grottoes consisted mainly of stone carvings but, as the quality of rocks in the Mogao Grottoes is not suitable for sculpture, the grottoes abound in clay sculptures.

Dazu Stone Sculptures First built in the seventh century in the early Tang Dynasty, the Dazu Stone Sculptures flourished in the Northern (960-1127) and Southern (1127-1279) Song dynasties. The

The Great Buddha Statue at Leshan, Sichuan.

Stone Treasure Stockade at Zhongxian, Chongqing.

The Huangze Temple at Guangyuan, Sichuan.

An old road built along the face of a cliff in Chengdu, Sichuan.

A panoramic view of the Dujiangyan Irrigation System in Sichuan, which was built 2,200 years ago.

Star-Observing Pavilion at White King Town, Chongqing.

A thatched pavilion resembling Du Fu's cottage in Chengdu, Sichuan.

Dazu stone sculpture art even extended to the Ming and Qing dynasties. It is located in the southeast of Sichuan Basin, 271 km from Chengdu, with Chongqing lying 167 km to its east. Though mainly consisting of Buddhist statues, the Dazu Stone Sculptures also depict some Confucian and Taoist figures. The exquisite sculptures display features of the late Buddhist sculpture art in China—humanized gods and deified humans.

Great Buddha Statue at Leshan Carving began in 713 and was completed 90 years later. Facing the roaring rapids of the Minjiang River, the Buddha statue looks graceful and sangfroid. The 71-meter-high statue can be viewed from many miles away. Its head is 14.7 meters long and 10 meters wide, two people can stand in its 7-meter-long ear, and over 100 can sit on its 8.5-meter-wide instep.

What most astonishes us is how the ancient people managed to keep it well proportioned without the aid of any scientific instrument. The statue has its own drainage system, composed of interlaced gutters set behind its ears and head. Storm-water drains away through these gutters to prevent the statue from being eroded by rain.

There are also many other grottoes with unique features in west China. Among them, the Xumi Mountain (Mt. Sumeru) Grottoes in Ningxia have a peculiar charm. Ridges and peaks of the mountain rise one after another, with exuberant woods and lovely murmuring brooks. Unlike most other grottoes, which were carved from one cliff, the Xumi Mountain Grottoes were chiseled out of cliffs of eight peaks, separated by wide gaps, in the Northern Wei (386-534), Sui (581-618), Tang, Song and Ming dynasties.

A province with the largest number of grottoes, Gansu now is home to nearly 100 of them. Apart from the Mogao Grottoes, the Maijishan Grottoes in Tianshui and the Yulin Grottoes in Anxi have won universal praise for their distinct glamour.

Famous Historic and Cultural Cities

Xi'an It was a great city in the eyes of Italian explorer Marco Polo. The oldest capital city in China, Xi'an has been dubbed one of the world's four great capital cities with an ancient civilization; the other three are Athens, Cairo and Rome. It was the capital city of 13 dynasties, including the Zhou (c.11th century-221 BC), Qin (221-207 BC), Han (206 BC-220) and Tang dynasties. During the Han and Tang

The Maijishan Grottoes.

The Lhableng Monastery in Gansu.

The Jiayuguan Pass in Gansu.

◄ A natural Buddha statue at the Beishan Buddhist Temple in Xining, Qinghai.

The Beishan Buddhist Temple in Xining City, Qinghai. ►

dynasties, it was China's political, economic, cultural and foreign exchange center, as well as the start of the Silk Road.

With a history of more than 3,100 years, Xi'an boasts rich cultural legacies. The city has 314 historic sites under special protection, and over 4,000 ruins and ancient tombs, plus more than 120,000 pieces of unearthed cultural relics. Among them, the Ming City Wall, the Qinshihuang Mausoleum and the Qin Terracotta Warriors and Horses are of great fame.

—Built in the Ming Dynasty, the Ming City Wall is the best-preserved ancient city wall in China, and the largest, best-preserved ancient military castle existing in the world. The wall is 13,912 meters in circumference, 12 meters high, 18 meters wide at the bottom and 15 meters wide at the top.

—The Qinshihuang Mausoleum, the tomb of the first emperor to unify China, is the largest of its kind so far found in the world. Located 35 km from Xi'an, building of it began in 247 BC, when Emperor Qinshihuang was enthroned, and it was completed in 209 BC, when the emperor passed away. Over 700,000 people were involved in its construction. The whole mausoleum covers 2.18 million square meters, 220,000 square meters of which were occupied by the tomb of the emperor. To preserve cultural relics, the Qinshihuang Mausoleum has not yet been excavated. Experts predict that a myriad of treasures would be found if its underground palaces are excavated.

—Situated 1.5 km east of the Qinshihuang Mausoleum, the Qin Terracotta Warriors and Horses are known as the "eighth wonder of the world". Over 8,000 dynamic terracotta warriors and horses form massive battle formations, presenting a true picture of the Qin army. Though similar in clothing and figure, as would be required by any army formation, the countenance, expressions, ages, hairstyles and even beards of the warrior figures are completely different. Every one of them is a delicate work of art.

Chengdu The 2,300-year-old Chengdu has created two miracles in Chinese history. One is that its name has remained unchanged for more than 2,000 years, a rare occurrence in China. The other is that it has been the capital city of Sichuan throughout its long history.

As the birthplace of ancient Shu Culture, Chengdu witnessed advanced development of the Bronze culture in the Shang (c.16th-11th century BC) and Zhou dynasties. Since the Han Dynasty, it had produced a group of remarkable literati and artists. The Tang and Song dynasties represented the cultural flourishing period for Chengdu; a shoal of renowned poets and painters resided here.

The Three Pagodas at Dali, Yunnan.

Qianxun Pagoda—One of
the Three Pagodas.

Xumi Mountain Grottoes.

The 72 Pagodas in Ningxia.

The Gaomiao Temple in Zhongwei, Ningxia.

A stone sculpture in front of the imperial tomb pictured below.

The Imperial Tombs of the Western Xia Regime (1038-1227) in Ningxia.

Its long history has left rich cultural relics and places of interest for Chengdu. There are over 100 historic sites under special protection, including the Marguis Wu Shrine, the Thatched Cottage of Du Fu and Dujiangyan Irrigation System.

—Great poet Du Fu (712-770) of the Tang Dynasty built a cottage by the Huanhua (Flower Bathing) Brook in the western outskirts of Chengdu when he wandered destitute to the city from the north. After reconstruction, today's Thatched Cottage of Du Fu, which covers 16 hectares, has elegant and simple structures and a quiet and beautiful courtyard. Du Fu accomplished brilliant achievements in composing poetry. Over 1,400 of his poems are still in existence.

—Situated on the Minjiang River in the west of Chengdu Plain, the well-known Dujiangyan Irrigation System, which was built 2,200 years ago by Li Bing, Chief of the Shu Prefecture of the State of Qin during the Warring States Period (475-221 BC), and his son, still functions well today. It is the oldest irrigation project in China and the only one in the world to channel water without a dam. Dujiangyan transformed Chengdu Plain, a victim of frequent floods and drought, into a land of plenty.

—Located in the outskirts of Chengdu, the famous Taoist mountain, Green City Mountain, appears to be in spring all year round, as its tall, ancient trees soar into the sky.

Lijiang At the foot of the snow-capped Yulong Mountain in northwest Yunnan, Lijiang is China's only ancient city without walls. The well-preserved city has been put onto the World Cultural Heritage List.

Surrounded by mountains, 800-year-old Lijiang was first built between the late 12th century and the early 13th century, and took shape in the Ming and Qing dynasties. The Ming and Qing structures along its streets were built of wood, stone and earth. Absorbing the architectural essence of the Naxi, Bai and Han ethnic groups, these free-style structures heed much to ornamentation. Rich-colored designs of birds and flowers were carved on windows and doors. Brooks run along Sifang Street and small alleys in the center of the city. Alleys paved with colored pebbles are neither sticky on rainy days nor dusty in summer. Ancient street-washing equipment is still in use, regularly cleaning the streets of the city.

Another special feature of Lijiang is Naxi music. Combining ancient Dongjing music with the folk music of the Naxi ethnic group, Naxi music is praised as "living music fossil". Naxi people still use the Dongba Script, the only remaining hieroglyphs in the world.

A painted mural in
the Dunhuang
Grottoes.

Exterior of the Mogao Grottoes at Dunhuang, Gansu.

The Genghis Khan Mausleum at Ih Ju League
in the Inner Mongolia Autonomous Region.

The Ghost Town in Xinjiang.

Ruins of the ancient city of Gaochang in Xinjiang.

The Emin Tower (Tower for Showing Gratitude for Eminhoja) in Turpan, Xinjiang, is the only one built in the unique Uygur architectural style in China.

The 11-Face, Thousand-Arm and Thousand-Eye Avalokitesvara (Goddess of Mercy) Statue in Tibet.

Ming (1368-1644) gold Buddha statue in Tibet.

Beautiful Landscape

China has a terraced terrain, which descends step by step from west to east. The third terrace consists of vast plains (Northeast China Plain, North China Plain and the plain in the middle and lower reaches of the Yangtze River), hills and low mountains, mostly less than 500 meters above sea level in height. The fourth terrace comprises the sub-littoral zones on the Chinese continental shelf. The western region spans the first and the second terrace.

The Qinghai-Tibet Plateau, with an average elevation of over 4,000 meters, forms the first terrace, the highest land on earth. Flanking the northern and eastern fringes of the world's largest and youngest land are the Kunlun, Qilian and Hengduan mountain ranges, which demarcate the first and the second terrace.

The second terrace consists of the Junggar Basin, the Tarim Basin, the Sichuan Basin, the Pamirs Plateau, the Inner Mongolia Plateau, the Loess Plateau, and the Yunnan-Guizhou Plateau. These landforms average 1,000 to 2,000 meters above sea level. The Greater Hinggan Mountains, Taihang Mountains, Wushan Mountain and Xuefeng Mountain, which fringe its eastern part, form a boundary line between the second and the third terrace.

Extending from east to west, the crescent-shaped Himalayan Mountain Range has an average elevation of over 6,000 meters. Gangdise Mountain lies parallel to its north, and it is bounded on the west by the Nyainqentanglha Mountains extending easterly to adjoin the Hengduan Mountains with a south-north trend. The Hengduan mountain system borders the Yunnan-Guizhou Plateau in the east. Towering high on the northern fringe of the Qinghai-Tibet Plateau, the Kunlun Mountain Range connects Northwest Sichuan Plateau and west Sichuan hilly area on the east, with Xinjiang—the center of the Eurasian Continent—at its northern end.

Because of its complicated geographical environment and diversified climatic conditions, the western region has multiple landforms, including deserts, pastureland, deep valleys, basins, lakes, glaciers, plateaus and polar mountain groups. These have nourished diverse types of natural vegetation, forming the region's unique ecological environment and producing many spectacular sights and wonders.

Yarlung Zangbo
Grand Canyon.

Yarlung Zangbo River.

Qomolangma Peak.

Mountains

Qomolangma Hundreds of millions of years ago, a mysterious land emerged from under the vast sea, and later developed into today's Qinghai-Tibet Plateau, known as the "roof of the world". It is freezing cold in most parts of the plateau, and mountains in and surrounding it are crowned with perpetual snow. The world's highest mountain, Qomolangma Peak, which towers 8,848.13 meters above sea level, is situated on the crest of the Himalayan range, with its pyramid-shaped summit shrouded in drifting white clouds. There are three huge glaciers on the northern slope of Qomolangma. In valleys of Qomolangma are tier upon tier ice peaks, forming a spectacular sight.

Established in 1989, the Qomolangma Nature Reserve is situated at the juncture of China's Tibet Autonomous Region and the Kingdom of Nepal, covering an area of 3.38 million hectares. It is the highest nature reserve in China. The 440-square-km Karmar Valley in the reserve rises 2,300 meters above sea level. Mostly covered by virgin forests, the reserve is home to 2,101 kinds of angiosperm plants, 50 species of beasts among other wild animals, more than 200 species of birds, and over 20 species of amphibians, reptiles and fish. The snow leopard is an indicative animal of the nature reserve. The area beyond the vast expanses of forests, at heights between 3,800 and 4,500 meters above sea level, is covered with alpine meadows, while the part above the snowline, rising 5,500 to 6,000 meters, is permanently covered with snow. The perpetual snow and ice accumulation evolved into glaciers, the longest stretching 22.2 km.

Qinling When the South China Sea was still a landmass and the Himalayas lay under the ocean, the Qinling Mountain Range already rose high into the clouds. It is a boundary between the northern and southern climatic zones in China. Its main peak, Taibai Mountain, is 3,767 meters above sea level. Among its numerous peaks, Tiantai Mountain is typical of the imposing manner of the range, which also boasts glaciers and perilous valleys. Tiantai Mountain is high and precipitous, with undulating and lofty mountain ridges. Lantian Mountain, with an elevation of 600 to 2,311 meters, encompasses a 3,645-hectare national forest park, and there is a plank road winding along the face of its steep cliffs.

Huashan, situated south of Huayin County, Shaanxi Province, is another famous mountain of the Qinling Mountain Range. One of the Five Sacred Mountains in China, it has an elevation of 2,160 meters.

The Salt Lake at Caka, Qinghai Province.

Bird Island in Qinghai Lake.

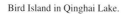

With bold cliffs, the towering Huashan has long been noted for its difficult accessibility, as just one rugged path leads to the summit. Now it has a second road, making the mountain more accessible. Huashan is a major place for Taoist activities. Many Taoist temples, buildings, terraces, huts and caves, constructed in distinctive styles, still remain.

Kunlun, Tianshan and Altay Mountains Traversing the northern fringe of the Qinghai-Tibet Plateau, the Kunlun Mountain Range stretches northerly to reach Xinjiang, which has a special terrain of its own. Altay Mountain towers high in its north, where the region's only river that flows into the sea runs through an undulating mountain pass. The 2,500-km-long Tianshan Mountain stretches across the central part of Xinjiang, dividing it into northern and southern parts. With different features, the two natural geographic regions respectively encompass the country's largest and second largest basin—Tarim Basin and Junggar Basin. The basins themselves are respectively encircled by China's largest and third largest desert—Taklimakan Desert and Gurbantunggut Desert.

Xinjiang's unique geographical environment is attributable to its spectacular, charming landscape. The three large mountain systems of Kunlun, Tianshan and Altay tower aloft in the region. Xinjiang boasts four of the world's 14 peaks that are over 8,000 meters above sea level. Qogir Peak in the western section of the Kunlun Mountains rises 8,611 meters above sea level, the second highest in the world. The three mountain systems have hundreds of peaks permanently covered with ice and snow, and their glaciers provide Xinjiang with rich ice reserves.

Snow water feeds the boundless expanses of virgin forests on both the southern and northern slopes of Tianshan Mountain and lush pasture in the vicinity. Beautiful lakes of different sizes are scattered about the mountain. Among them, Tianchi Lake (or Heavenly Lake) is the most wonderful. An alpine lake in the embrace of Tianshan Mountain, Tianchi is formed of snowmelt water, with a depth of nearly 100 meters. In mid-summer, surrounding fields are carpeted with green and luxuriant grass, dotted with blooming flowers. It is a special treat to stand by the lakeside and look toward the distant snow-capped mountain peaks. Viewed from top of a mountain, Tianchi, with reflections of distant mountains in its clear water, appears exceptionally enchanting. In winter, the area becomes a world of snow, and an ideal natural alpine ski field.

Bogda Peak in Xinjiang.▲
Sayram Lake in Xinjiang.▶

The beautiful scenery of Tianchi, or Heavenly Lake, under snow.

Snow lotus *(Saussurea involucrate)* growing on ice-capped mountains in Xinjiang.

Snow-crowned Tianshan Mountain in Xinjiang.

Hanas Lake nestles in the virgin forests on Altay Mountain. It is the deepest alpine lake in China, with its deepest section of 188.4 meters. It is also a mysterious lake, as the color of its water changes with the effects of sunlight and in different seasons. Between the arbor woods and meadows surrounding the lake, a variety of flora grows distinctly distributed on different heights of the mountain. Brown bear, red deer and musk deer haunt the area and schools of taimen salmon, known as "red river monsters", swim in the lake, stirring the calm and smooth water surface. When ascending a mountain during July and August, you can enjoy the wonderful sight of "Buddha's Aureole", especially in the days after rain. The lake water flows into Burqin River, and there are several villages along riverbanks. The villagers' primitive wooden houses and yurts, and their peaceful and easy country life, are in perfect harmony with the charming scenery of Hanas Lake.

Snow water from the three large mountain systems has also created other beautiful lakes, including the picturesque Bayanbulak Swan Lake and Bosten—the largest inland freshwater lake in China.

Emei Mountain Situated in the southwest of Sichuan Basin, Emei Mountain is widely noted for incorporating beautiful landscape and Buddhist culture. It is a tourist attraction that has been included in the World Natural and Cultural Heritage List.

The mountain has been renowned for its lovely scenery since ancient times. Green ridges roll in undulating waves; springs and waterfalls are seen everywhere; and graceful peaks occasionally become visible from behind rifted clouds. Under the surging sea of clouds are bottomless chasms. The mountain is also important for its unique geological features and well-preserved ecosystem. It is known as a graphic geological museum for its special strata, a flora museum for its diversified vegetation, and a museum of Buddhist culture and ancient Chinese architecture.

Emei is called "Guangming (Brightness) Mountain" by Buddhists. According to a legend, the Guangxiang Temple on its summit was where Samantabhadra, Bodhisattva of Universal Benevolence, preached Buddhism. During its heyday, the mountain had more than 100 temples, nunneries and halls, of which some 20 still remain. Baoguo Temple is the largest of its kind, sitting at the foot of the mountain.

You can enjoy three wonderful views from the summit of Emei Mountain—sunrise, a sea of clouds

Snow-capped Qilian Mountain, deserts and grasslands form a unique landscape in the western part of the Hexi Corridor in Gansu.

and Buddha's Aureole. If you stand at the edge of Sheshen (Sacrifice) Cliff between three and four o'clock in the afternoon, with the sun behind you, you can see a rainbow ring in a cloudbank below the summit, with your shadow in the center of the ring. This rainbow ring has been known as "Buddha's Aureole". It is said that in ancient times, people thought they had predestined ties with Buddha when they saw the ring; many jumped down the precipice without hesitation, thinking they would immediately become immortal. Hence, this 600-meter precipice was named Sacrifice Cliff.

Scientists say that this rainbow ring is actually a natural phenomenon due to the refraction of sunlight.

Fanjing Mountain Covering 567 square km, Fanjing Mountain is one of the areas in China that preserves a comparatively complete subtropical forest ecosystem. It boasts the most intact virgin forests compared with other places in the world on the same latitude. It is considered to be an ancient landmass that formed 1-1.4 billion years ago. There are more than 2,600 species of fauna and flora, including many Tertiary and Quaternary species existing 70 million to 2 million years ago. Therefore, the place is famed as a rare ecological kingdom.

As early as in the 16th century, Fanjing Mountain in northeast Guizhou became a sacred Buddhist place in China. In the 20th century, scientists found that the mountain is the only habitat of the Guizhou golden monkey—a rare animal species native to China.

Living in dense forests and deep mountains 1,400 meters above sea level, the Guizhou golden monkey is a species on the verge of extinction. There are just 750 such monkeys still existing in the world today. The monkey has a blue face, an upturned nose, a long tail, dark gray limbs, and glossy gray long hair all over its body. As they mainly live in the upper part of high trees, the monkeys are quick in climbing trees and good at jumping. They usually live and move about in groups consisting of dozens of monkeys.

Due to their small number and limited area of habitat, not much scientific data about them are available. The Convention on International Trade in Endangered Species of Wild Fauna and Flora lists the monkey as an E-class, the highest grade, of animal species for protection. No zoo, anywhere in the world, has successfully raised or exhibited the monkey.

The Ashartu Stone Forest, formed from the Quaternary glacier, in the Inner Mongolia Autonomous Region.

A nature reserve in Inner Mongolia.

Rivers

Yarlung Zangbo   The Tibetan ethnic group regards the Yarlung Zangbo River as its "cradle" and "mother river". It is the longest river in Tibet, extending 2,091 km in the boundaries of China. Meaning "snow water from high mountains" in Tibetan, the river originates in the northern foothills of the Himalayas, rushing through the southern part of the Qinghai-Tibet Plateau. Gathering water from many tributaries, the river widens while flowing on its downward path. When it reaches the juncture of Mainling and Medog counties in east Tibet, Namjagbarwa, the highest peak in the eastern section of the Himalayas, blocks its way. The river has to change the direction of its course, resulting in the emergence of a world wonder, the U-shaped Yarlung Zangbo Grand Canyon, which is 504.6 km long. The river is sandwiched by two precipitous peaks, soaring 7,782 meters and 7,234 meters above sea level respectively on its southern and northern banks. The greatest distance from the summit of a peak to the surface of the river is 5,382 meters, while it is a mere 74 meters wide at the narrowest part at the bottom of the canyon. It deserves its fame as the world's No.1 canyon, as it beats in length and depth both the Colorado Grand Canyon in the United States and the Colca Canyon in Peru.

The Yangtze and Yellow Rivers   Both rivers have their sources in Qinghai Province. The Yangtze originates in the Geladaindong, the main peak of the Tanggula Mountains, which rises 6,548 meters above sea level. There is a vast expanse of seracs on the glacier. Their melted water forms the headstream of the Yangtze River. Towering tens of meters, the seracs appear like crystal pinnacles in diverse forms, creating gorgeous scenery at the river source. Besides its beautiful scenery, the place has rich natural resources, including rock crystal and magnetic iron ore. It abounds in alepidote (a fish without scales) and snow cock, as well as animals such as the wild ass, white-lipped deer, wild yak and snow leopard.

The Yellow River rises from its source in an oval-shaped basin at the northern foot of Bayan Har Mountain. More than 100 small lakes are scattered like stars over the basin, which measures 40 km from east to west and 60 km from south to north. Spring water, gushing out of a 4-square-meter fountain in the southwest of the basin, joins other brooks to form the Maqu River, source stream of the Yellow River, which is 10 meters wide and 0.5 meters deep. The Yellow River's source averages an elevation of over 4,000

Shahu Lake in Ningxia.

Autumn scenery of Liupan Mountain in Ningxia.

51

Hukou Waterfall in the Yellow River at Yichuan, Shaanxi Province.

1. A sheepskin raft—a popular method used in west China to carry people across the Yellow River.
2.The Yellow River winds through Ningxia.

3. Landscape of the Loess Plateau in Shaanxi.
4. Huashan Mountain in Shaanxi.

meters. Lush meadows, together with the scattered lakes and brooks, form beautiful landscapes, and the place has been listed as a national nature reserve, the largest of its kind in the world.

Yellow River Attractions Flowing across extensive grasslands in Gonghe County, Qinghai, the Yellow River comes to the embouchure of the first gorge on its course. The embouchure is a mere 30 meters wide, with steep-sided granite rocks standing 200 meters on both sides. It is an ideal place to build a dam, so Longyangxia Reservoir was built here. Its 178-meter-high dam is so far the highest in China and the reservoir has a storage capacity of 24.7 billion cubic meters. With such a huge storage capacity, the reservoir has functioned well in regulating the water flow of the Yellow River during dry seasons. Its power generation is next only to that of Gezhouba and Baishan hydropower stations. Longyangxia Reservoir represents the first spectacle on the upper reaches of the Yellow River.

The magnificent view reappears as the river reaches Yongjing, Gansu. High mountains and towering ridges roll along its banks, forming a deep gorge. A huge dam, 840 meters long and 147 meters high, was built to block the flow of the river. This is Liujiaxia Reservoir, with a storage capacity of 5.7 billion cubic meters and a 130 square km water surface.

Exiting Gansu, the river enters the Ningxia Plain. With its bed widening, the river becomes gentler, but starts to get muddy as it brings along desert sand, including that of the Tengger Desert, which is situated along its banks. The famous Shapotou "Sand Control Park" was built along the riverside at the juncture of the Tengger Desert and Xiushan Mountain Range. The railway from Baotou of Inner Mongolia to Lanzhou of Gansu passes through the southeastern fringe of the Tengger Desert. To guarantee smooth transportation, Chinese sand control experts have created a miracle here. Through years of effort, they built a 500-meter-wide "green wall" along both sides of the railway, which stretches 45 km.

Along the northern bank of the Yellow River west of Zhongwei County, Ningxia, is another desert attraction—Mingshashan, or the Singing Sand Dune. Sliding down from top of the dune on sunny days you can hear a booming sound, like the rolling of drums. A legend says it is because an ancient castle was buried under the sand dune, while scientists say the sound is produced by friction generated when the quartz sand grains move.

The river then enters Shaanxi. At Hukou Township, Yichuan County, the riverbed abruptly narrows

Jiuzhaigou in Sichuan Province is famous for its beautiful natural landscape.

Huanglong (Yellow Dragon) Scenic Spot in Sichuan.

into trough 20-30 meters wide, and the current becomes faster. The turbulent current rolls thunderously down into a big stone-strewn pool, forming a 20-meter-high waterfall and producing thick mist. The sight resembles boiling water poured from a flask, hence the name of the waterfall—Hukou (Flask Mouth) Waterfall. Its rumbling sound can be heard miles away.

Three Gorges of the Yangtze River Flowing downward in rushing rapids from the Qinghai-Tibet Plateau, the Yangtze River admits the waters of dozens of rivers, including the Jialing, Wujiang and Daning rivers, on its way to the sea. Leaving the western highlands behind, the river enters the most beautiful part of its course at Chongqing, the Three Gorges area, which is famed as an "art gallery of landscape". From Baidi (White King) Town at Fengjie County of Chongqing in the west to Nanjinguan in Yichang City of Hubei Province in the east, the Yangtze flows for 193 km through the three gorges of Qutang, Wuxia and Xiling. The 8-km Qutang Gorge is noted for its magnificent and enchanting scenery. Baiyan Mountain and Chijia Mountain, with their steep, sheer slopes, stand facing each other on both sides of the river. Containing many rapids and eddies, the roaring waves of the river roll past the gorge. Exiting Qutang Gorge, the river winds through the narrow, zigzagging Wuxia Gorge, which stretches 44 km. The deep gorge is well known for its quiet, graceful environment, especially its 12 towering exotic peaks enshrouded in mist. Located in Hubei Province, the 76-km Xiling Gorge features many shoals and rapids, and numerous reefs. Besides its beautiful landscape, the Three Gorges area also has many cultural relics dating back to the Three Kingdoms period in the third century, as well as other historical sites, old structures and rich folklore.

Grassland and Plateau

North Tibet Grassland The vast North Tibet Grassland lies between the Kunlun, Gangdise and Nyainqentanglha mountains in the north of the Qinghai-Tibet Plateau.

Due to its high elevation and frigid weather, the 400,000-square-km North Tibet Grassland is an untraversed area, thus becoming a paradise for wildlife and one of the largest natural zoos in the world. Wild asses, yaks and antelopes live and reproduce here leisurely and carefree. The wild antelope is the

A Taoist temple on Qingcheng Mountain.

Qingcheng (Green City) Mountain in Sichuan is a sacred Taoist place.

most popular animal, and generally dozens of antelopes live together. In mating season, thousands of antelopes gather together on the grassland, with their beautiful long horns waving up and down, presenting a spectacular sight. The wild yak is the most stalwart animal on the North Tibet Grassland. Strong and big, some even weigh up to 1,000 kg. Wild asses are gallopers, and often migrate in large groups. The grassland is also the habitat of more than 100 other species of rare wild animals, such as the black-necked crane, snow leopard, argali and brown panda.

Inner Mongolia Grassland The Inner Mongolia Grassland is a natural pastureland in China, where more than 10 ethnic minority groups, including Mongolian, Manchu, Hui, Daur, Ewenki and Oroqen, live. They mostly engage in animal breeding, and each ethnic group has their own customs. Together, they contribute to the rich, diversified folklore of the Inner Mongolia Grassland. Having a pleasant climate in summer, the grassland is an ideal summer resort. The annual Nadam Fair is a traditional Mongolian event, during which Mongolian young people stage wrestling and horse racing contests.

West Sichuan Plateau An extensive grassland extends several thousand square kilometers at the juncture where the Qinghai-Tibet Plateau meets the Hengduan Mountain Range. It sharply contrasts with the surrounding lofty mountains and perilous valleys. Here is the West Sichuan Plateau, which has a terrain descending from north to south because of the south-north trend of the Hengduan Mountains. As such a terrain enables the southwesterly and southeasterly marine monsoon to reach through the zigzagging river valleys, the plateau abounds in precipitation, and is covered with a carpet of green grass and luxuriant plants. The main peak of Gonggar Mountain rises 7,590 meters above sea level, 55 km south of the Kangding County in the Garze Tibetan Autonomous Prefecture on the plateau. The highest peak in Sichuan Province, it is perpetually covered with ice and snowfields. Hailuogou (Conch Gully) Glacier Forest Park at the foot of the mountain is winning the increasing favor of tourists. Conch Gully has glaciers with the lowest elevation, compared with other places on the same latitude elsewhere in the world. What is even more wonderful is that a boiling spring exists in this world of ice and snow, with a water temperature as high as 90 degrees Celsius. Visitors can enjoy bathing in the hot spring, with glaciers all around them.

Loess Plateau The Loess Plateau stretches from the Qinling Mountains in the south to Yinshan

Sailing past Wushan Mountain.

Kuimen—west entrance of the Three
Gorges of the Yangtze River.

Scenery at the Small Three Gorges of Daning
River at Wushan.

Huangguoshu Waterfall in Guizhou.

Dragon Palace, a 15-km-long karst cave, in Guizhou Province.

A masterpiece of nature—Mushroom Rock on top of Fanjing Mountain in Guizhou.

Mountain in the north, with Shaanxi and Ningxia situated on it. The plateau is formed of fine loess soil brought here by strong northwesterly winds from Central Asia and Mongolia over the past million years. Ensuing weathering has created the plateau's wonderful and unique scenery of loess highlands, loess ridges and loess hills. The plateau is a birthplace of ancient farming culture. It typically features washout gullies, ravines, and row upon row of dwelling caves with doors and windows decorated with primitive patterns of paper-cuts. Tracts of farm fields resemble an artist's palette, presenting remarkably identical colors.

Gully and Valley

Shangri-La So-called "Shangri-La" is situated in the Deqen Tibetan Autonomous Prefecture, northwest Yunnan Province. Covering 23,870 square km, the prefecture borders on Tibet. Here, the Jinsha River, the upstream of the Yangtze River, the Lancang River, the upstream of the Mekong River, and Nujiang, the upstream of Salween River, rush down southward from the Qinghai-Tibet Plateau. The three rivers flow parallel, forming a magnificent scene.

The special geographical environment of Shangri-La created its marvelous natural landscape. From the Jinsha River banks, with features typical of south China, to the snow-capped mountains, visitors can enjoy scenery of the world's different climatic zones within one day. In the scorching heat of mountain valley floor, verdant woods and fruit plants grow. The temperate cool mountain slopes are covered with green grass and beautiful flowers, while the frigid mountain summit is a world of crystal ice and snow. With a prominent vertical climate, the place has abundant flora, fauna and microorganism resources. There are over 5,000 species of seed plants, including many precious medicinal herbs and rare ornamental plants. It is home to 89 species of mammals, some of which have been listed as animals under first-class State protection, including the Yunnan golden monkey, wild ass, snow leopard *(Panthera uncia)*, leopard *(Panthera pardus)* and goral. There are 170 species of wild birds, including some under first-class State protection, such as the black-necked crane. Shangri-La also abounds in flora, featuring over 200 species of azalea. Precious flowers and plants, such as the orchid, Saussurea involucrata, radix gentianae and lily, are

The Hutiao Gorge of Jinsha River in Yunnan Province.

The First Bend of the Yangtze River.

widely distributed here.

Some Chinese minority ethnic groups that have small numbers of people live together in Shangri-La. They include the Lisu, Nu, Derung and Pumi ethnic groups. These groups have their own cultures, customs and festivals, as well as varying colorful costumes, and form another attraction of Shangri-La.

Jiuzhaigou Jiuzhaigou nestles in the mountains at the juncture of Nanping, Songpan and Pingwu counties in the Aba Tibetan-Qiang Autonomous Prefecture, north Sichuan. Covering 620 square km, it is a mountain gully stretching for more than 40 km. It incorporates the beautiful natural scenes of lakes, waterfalls, snow-capped mountains and forests. The place, sparsely inhabited, has a primitive natural beauty, thus being famed as a "fairyland".

A total of 108 beautiful alpine lakes are scattered throughout Jiuzhaigou, with the smallest less than 0.5 *mu* in size and the longest stretching for 7.5 km. The lakes here contain large amounts of calcium carbonate. As a result, their beds and brink are paved with calcium carbonate crystals. The water is so clear that you can see to the bottom of the lakes, though they are generally tens of meters deep. Waterfalls are the essence of Jiuzhaigou scenery. Countless trickles flow from woods-covered cliffs and shoals, forming larger streams. Some flow slowly and smoothly, while others rush rapidly.

The gully also boasts virgin forests and features big temperature differences. A variety of plants are distributed vertically at different heights. Lower mountain slopes are covered with broad-leaved forests, while upper slopes feature coniferous forests. In autumn, the snow-covered mountain summit sharply contrasts with the multi-colored mountain slopes and base.

Lakes

Qinghai Lake Located 180 km from Xining, capital of Qinghai Province, Qinghai Lake is the largest inland saltwater lake in China, with about 20 percent salt content. It has been included in the List of Wetlands of International Importance and Convention on Wetlands of International Importance Especially as a Waterfowl Habitat.

With an elevation of 3,196 meters, the lake covers 4,583 square km and is 360 km in circumference,

Lugu Lake in Yunnan is a deep and unpolluted highland lake.

The Stone Forest in Yunnan.

the deepest part of which reaches 32.8 meters. Its main attraction, Bird Island, is the most gorgeous of the five islands in the lake. Situated in the northwest of the lake, Bird Island covers 0.8 square km. A home for birds of different species, the island greets over 100,000 birds, including the brown-headed gulls, wild geese, cormorants, swans and ducks, migrating from south China and Southeast Asia from late March to early April each year. Birds hover in the sky over the small island, which is covered by multifarious nests and eggs. The gay sound of the birds carries for many miles, and it has become a bird-breeding site with the largest density in Asia. In winter, the birds flock back to the south.

Caohai Lake　Near the Weining Yi-Hui-Miao Autonomous County of Guizhou Province, Caohai Lake covers about 20 square km, with an elevation of 2,200 meters. Luxuriant trees and lush grass surround this natural plateau lake, which is also a national bird protection zone. Its unique natural environment and ecosystem have attracted more than 140 species of migrant and resident birds, including the black-necked crane, white-fronted goose and red-crowned crane. Caohai Lake boasts pleasant weather. Seen from afar on days of gentle breezes and bright sunshine, the lake appears to merge with the horizon far beyond.

Namco and Lakes in Tibet　More than 100 lakes are scattered over the North Tibet Grassland like handfuls of sparkling jewels. Of them, Namco is the largest lake in Tibet, covering 1,920 square km. It is also the highest lake in the world, at a height of 4,718 meters above sea level. "Namco" means "Heavenly Lake" in Tibetan. With the azure sky and snow-capped mountain peaks reflected in its clear water, Namco looks exceptionally quiet, secluded and holy. In winter, the lake is frozen. When it begins to thaw in early summer, the cracking sounds of its ice are deafening. In mid-summer, flocks of fish freely swim in the lake.

Tibetans regard Mapam Yumco in Ngari as a "Holy Lake". Each year, a large number of pilgrims and tourists from Nepal and India come here on pilgrimage. Yamzhog Yumco, noted for its graceful scenery, lies quietly between snow-capped mountains. In the fields beside the lake, cows and sheep grow strong, fed with lush grass. Flocks of swans and ruddy sheldrakes inhabit islands in the lake.

Shangri-La Canyon in Yunnan.

Baishuitai—A holy place for Naxi people.

Snow-capped Meili Mountain in Yunnan.

"Moon Canyon" on the upper reaches
of Lancang River in Yunnan.

Highland meadows in Yunnan.

69

Hometown of Giant Pandas

Excavation findings have proved that giant pandas were carnivores in primeval times, widely distributed throughout the planet. At that time, the ecological environment differed greatly from what it is like today. Huge geomorphologic changes in the late Mesozoic era exerted their forces on almost everything: Seawaters retreated, mountains protruded, most gymnosperms disappeared and fauna was buried underground, leaving only fossils behind. However, giant pandas miraculously survived, albeit with different habits. Rather than ferocious carnivores wandering the Earth, they are now tender bamboo-eaters living in remote forests.

Today, giant pandas mainly live in Minshan, Qionglai, Daxiang and Xiaoxiang mountains in northwest Sichuan, as their special ecosystem renders them a comfortable home for giant pandas. Here, exuberant virgin forests block the sunlight, lush green bamboo and thickets cover the mountains, and brooks gurgle underfoot. To protect this species now with only 1,000 giant pandas living in the wild, China has established the four nature reserves of Wolong, Fengtongzhai, Tangjiahe and Wanglang. Wolong Nature Reserve has been listed in theUN's Man and Biosphere Program.

Karst Wonders

The Yunnan-Guizhou Plateau is composed of Yunnan and Guizhou provinces. Most of China's karst landforms are found in the plateau as well as in adjacent Sichuan and Guangxi. Corrosion during tens of millions of years has created a myriad of limestone caves and miraculous wonders of open karst topographies.

Dragon Palace Located 132 km from Guiyang, capital of Guizhou Province, the Dragon Palace is actually a 15-km-long limestone cave, passing through more than 20 mountains and linking over 90 caves. The longest limestone cave in China, the Dragon Palace teems with fantastic scenes of underground lakes, waterfalls, stone forests and cliffs.

Zhijin Cave Located in Zhijin County, Guizhou, Zhijin Cave stretches for some 10 km, and the highest part is 100 meters. Owing to its complex stratigraphic structure, the cave contains numerous exotic stalactites. It is the world's best-preserved limestone cave with the most beautiful formations. A 17-meter-

Detian Waterfall
in Guangxi.

Picturesque Lijiang scenery at Guilin, Guangxi.

high column inside the cave appears to have been formed by layers of crystal-clear glossy ganodermas. It is already 240,000 years old according to geologists.

Huangguoshu Waterfall Without seeing it with your own eyes, you could never imagine how a limestone cave that collapsed due to water erosion can form a 71-meter-high waterfall. Some 60 km south of Anshun, Guizhou, Huangguoshu Waterfall is the largest of the 22 falls formed due to the sinking of the bed of Baishui River. Nearly 40 meters wide, the roaring water of the waterfall pours down the cliff with a thunderous sound. Behind the fall lies the 134-meter-long Water Curtain Cave. You can watch the grand waterfall from inside the cave, which makes you feel as if you are in a fairyland.

Stone Forest Covering 350 square km and lying 86 km from Kunming, capital of Yunnan, the Stone Forest is another of China's typical karst topography. It presents a vision of what it was like at bottom of the sea 270 million years ago. Here, stones carved by nature have an infinite variety of shapes. Corroded depressions, and underground rivers and limestone caves are scattered about. Huge stone columns and pinnacles of varying heights ascend to the sky, blocking the sunlight.

Huanglongsi Scenic Spot Abutting the Jiuzhaigou Scenic Spot in Sichuan, the Huanglongsi Scenic Spot has been noted for its exotic scenery of open-air stalactites and the 3.6-km-long light yellow-colored Huanglong (Yellow Dragon) Gully. Up to 70 meters wide, the gully, abundant with bright yellow calcified rocks, zigzags like a huge golden dragon, hence its name. Under geological influence, the limestone stratum formed into several karst lakes adjacent to each other. With sediments from a variety of minerals, the bottom of the lakes sparkles like jewels and the crystal-clear water glitters with jade-like stalactites at the bank of the lakes.

Guilin Landscape Thanks to its picturesque scenery, Guilin in northeast Guangxi seems more famous than the regional capital city Nanning. Originating in Mao'er (Cat's Ear) Mountain in north Guilin, the 82-km-long section of the Lijiang River from Guilin to Yangshuo winds its way among karst mountains, forming the famous picturesque Guilin landscape. Along the river, grotesque stones are scattered, some shaped like humans and others resembling beasts. It is estimated that there are over 2,000 underground limestone caves along the riverbanks, containing numerous stalactites and stalagmites.

Altun Mountain Nature Reserve
is a paradise for wild asses.

Tropical rainforests in Xishuangbanna,
Yunnan, are the home of wild elephants.

Ferocious carnivores in primeval times, giant
pandas are now tender bamboo-eaters.

A golden monkey.

Religions and Folk Customs

Many of the country's 56 ethnic groups inhabit west China. Their simple and pristine customs and unique regional culture, including farming, festivals, food, clothing and languages, plus the impressive western scenery, present a rich picture of Chinese folk customs.

Religions are part of the special charm of this region. Formed in the second century, Taoism is indigenous to China, while Buddhism and Islam were brought into the country from India and Arab countries over 1,000 years ago. Over 10 ethnic groups believe in Islam, including the Hui and Uygur people. There are quite a few faithful Buddhist ethnic groups, including Tibetans and Dai people. Others are devotees of some primitive religions.

Religion

Religion has exerted an influence on Chinese politics, economy, social life, culture and arts, music and dance, architecture and even people's way of thinking, leaving a multitude of religious structures all over the country.

Buddhism Popular in Tibet, Buddhism in the region has its own features. As there are large numbers of followers, the region boasts many monasteries.

Combining the features of a palace, castle and monastery, the world-famous Potala Palace is considered the symbol of typical Tibetan architecture. Lying 3,700 meters above sea level in the northwest of Lhasa, capital of Tibet Autonomous Region, the Potala Palace covers 41 hectares. The 13-story main building, 115 meters high, is a complete stone and wood structure. Built in the seventh century, it was originally for the use of Princess Wencheng of the Tang Imperial Court, who married the Tubo King Songtsam Gambo. It later became the residence of Dalai Lamas, a place where they dealt with political affairs and a site where their remains are enshrined.

The Jokhang Monastery in the center of Lhasa covers 25,100 square meters and has over 20 halls.

Manjusri Buddha Statue of Tar Monastery in Huangzhong County, Qinghai.

Baoguo Temple at the foot of Emei Mountain hosts an activity
in front of the Maitreya Hall to set captive animals free.

Songtsanling Monastery, the largest Tibetan Buddhist complex in Yunnan.

A Buddhist service is held at Langmu Monastery, Gansu.

A service at the Dongguan
Mosque in Xining, Qinghai.

The Great Mosque in Ningxia.

These buildings at Qinglongdong, Guizhou, are famous Taoist structures built in the Ming Dynasty (1368-1644).

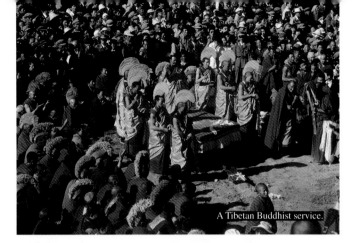
A Tibetan Buddhist service.

A religious ritual held at Tar Monastery.

Integrating features of Nepalese and Indian architecture, the monastery is quite magnificent and gorgeous. The Tashilhungpo Monastery in Xigaze, Tibet, has been the residence of the Panchen Lama since the Fourth Panchen Erdeni. It consists of the hall, Abbot Conference (the highest organ of the local government of former rear Tibet), a memorial hall for stupas for remains of Panchen Lamas and a sutra school. The main sutra hall can accommodate 2,000 lamas to chant sutras. The 30-meter-high Maitreya Hall houses a seated bronze statue of Maitreya Buddha. With a height of 26.2 meters, it is one of the largest bronze statues in the world.

The Tar Monastery in Huangzhong, Qinghai, is one of the six major monasteries of the Gelug (Yellow) Sect in Tibetan Buddhism. It has three unique art specialties—mural, padded flowers made from satin of different colors and colored butter designs. The butter designs are graphic, with vivid figurines, trees and flowers, birds and animals made from butter.

Islam Many ethnic groups, including the Uygur, Mongol, Hui, Kazak, Uzbek and Russian, inhibit Xinjiang. Most Uygur people believe in Islam, thus, the mosques in Xinjiang are very magnificent. The Aitga Mosque in Kashi is the largest of its kind in Xinjiang. Covering over 16,000 square meters, it is flanked by two 10-meter-high turrets. With a chapel capable of hosting up to 7,000 devotees, the mosque is not only the center for Islamic activities in Xinjiang but also a major place for people to celebrate the Corban Festival and Festival of Fast-breaking.

In Ningxia, the mosques of the Hui people, who are also Muslims, are stately and imposing, with spacious halls. The Nanguan Mosque in Yinchuan, the capital city of Ningxia, stands tall and erect, displaying distinct features of Islamic architecture. Its hall can house over 1,000 people. Tongxin Mosque in Tongxin County is the largest remaining example of Islamic structure in Ningxia, incorporating traditional brick carving techniques of the Han people with Islamic architectural art.

Folk Customs

Uygur Uygur people, who mainly live in Xinjiang, have the largest population among ethnic groups in the region and are famous for their talents in singing and dancing.

1. Tibetan people celebrate the Giant Tangka Displaying Ceremony.

2. Tibetan people at Tongren County, Qinghai, celebrate an ethnic festival.

3. Totems popular in North Tibet Grassland.

A Tibetan woman.

Tibetan people in splendid ethnic attire.

A food street in Xi'an.

A courtyard cave residence built in the late
Qing Dynasty (1644-1911) in Mizhi, Shaanxi.

Shaanxi is famous for the Ansai waist drum dance.

They favor almond hats, just as the preference of Uzbek people for cotton and Koreans for the azalea. A mother will give her daughter an almond hat to show her deep fondness for the girl, and girls will send this hat to their sweethearts as a symbol of love.

Tibetan Mostly living in Tibet, the Tibetan people also inhibit Qinghai, Gansu and Sichuan and all have similar customs.

Tibetan people have many traditional festivals. Their New Year's Day, the first day of the Tibetan calendar that began in 1027, is the grandest. During this festival, family members stay together, sending best wishes to each other. The Monlam or Grand Summons Ceremony, the greatest of all Tibetan religious festivals, takes place from the third to the 24th day of the first month of each Tibetan lunar year. During the period, 20,000 lamas from the three major monasteries in Tibet gather in the Jokhang Monastery, praying to the statue of Sakyamuni and taking part in Buddhist academic degree exams. Buddhist believers from Tibet and other places come to pay homage to Buddha and give donations. The Shoton Festival is one of the most interesting ones. In the past, relatives of Buddhists took sour milk up to the mountain to celebrate their completion of the practice of Buddhism. On their way home, they drank the milk, singing and dancing. Hence the Shoton Festival is also known as the Sour Milk Drinking Festival. It has been designated as the festival of Tibetan opera since the 17th century. In five days from the 30th day of the sixth month of each Tibetan lunar year, Tibetan opera troupes gather at Norbu Linka in Lhasa to perform and compete against one another.

Hui Though widely distributed in China, the Hui people mainly inhibit Ningxia, Qinghai and Gansu. Flowers are the theme of their popular folk songs, which have fixed tunes. Girls are usually compared to beautiful flowers and handsome young men to youngsters. Though mainly about love between men and women, songs also present anecdotes, legends, and unusual customs.

Dai Pristine Dai people live in affluent Xishuangbanna of Yunnan Province. The ancient Buddhist temples, bamboo stilt houses and Dai girls in florid straight skirts enhance each other.

Their Water-Sprinkling Festival, occurring annually on April 13-15, is the most influential event in Yunnan. During the three days, Dai girls dress in splendid attire and young men are wreathed in smiles.

Yugur women in splendid ethnic attire.

Mongol wrestlers.

Karez—An irrigation system of wells connected by underground channels, popular in Xinjiang.

This Uygur elderly is drying grapes.

A woman of the Hui ethnic group.

A Kazakh woman and her children.

Jino people in Yunnan celebrate a festival.

A young woman of the Qiang ethnic group.

93

Everyone carries fresh water to sprinkle on Buddha statues in temples and then on each other. Water splashing in the air presents a scene of happiness.

Miao An old ethnic group, the Miao in Guizhou are the second largest group of people next only to the Han in the province. Over 60 percent of the Miao people live in Guizhou, mainly the areas in Miaoling Mountain and along Qingshui River in the southeast. The Miao also live in compact communities in Sichuan, Yunnan and Chongqing.

There are special dating customs for Miao young people. Since ancient times, this ethnic group has had a strange tradition of escaping marriage. The runaway bride would not see the groom for three days, living in the groom's relatives' home. Elders in high esteem would then go to the bride's home to persuade her to marry the groom.

Accompanied by the *Lusheng* (reed-pipe wind instrument) and songs, Miao people are also noted for their dexterity. They are good at handcrafts, including exquisite embroidered clothing, complicated silver headdress worn only on festivals and wax printing.

Yi Mainly distributed in Sichuan and Yunnan, the Yi people believe that everything is intelligent, and they worship their ancestors. Closely connected to fire, the Yi people are famous for their Torchlight Festival. During the daytime on the 24th day of the sixth month of each Chinese lunar year, men take part in bullfighting, horseracing and wrestling, while women sing and whistle. At night, every family will hold a torch around their house before gathering on hills, where they play till dawn.

Mosuo The mysterious Mosuo people live by Lugu Lake, which has an elevation of 2,860 meters.

Situated between Ninglang Yi Autonomous County of Yunnan and Yanyuan County of Sichuan, Lugu Lake is more than 270 km from the ancient city of Lijiang. Covering 51.8 square km, the lake is 40.3 meters deep, with the deepest part 93.5 meters. One of the deepest freshwater lakes in China, it is among the few unpolluted lakes in the world.

The lake is surrounded by hills, with faintly discernible small islands. Its banks meander and have several open sandy beaches. Seen during different time of the day, its clear water shines with different

A girl of the Ke, a branch of the Miao ethnic group in Guizhou.

Miao girls.

A child of the Zhuang ethnic group.

A happy couple of the Changjiao Miao, a branch of the Miao ethnic group.

Happy newlyweds of the Hani ethnic group.

Famous Guizhou wax printing.

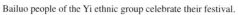

Bailuo people of the Yi ethnic group celebrate their festival.

Villagers of a Bouyei village in Guizhou celebrate a festive occasion.

colors: In the morning, the sun suffuses the lake with golden yellow; when the sun rises up slowly, the water changes to emerald green, and becomes deep green at sunset.

Good-looking Mosuo girls can be seen here. Their demeanor, the lovely canoes and the melodious fisherman's songs are regarded as the three specialties in the Lugu Lake area.

The Mosuo people also keep the rare custom of being a matrilineal clan. Elder or capable women are the head of the family. Men and women live in their mother's home, never marrying each other. At the age of 13, a "trousers or skirts wearing" ceremony will be held, a symbol of maturity. Then, they can participate in the social life and make intimate friends.

Once a man and a woman fall in love with each other, the man will send her gold, silver or jade jewelry, beads or silk ribbons, taking into account his own financial conditions. The woman will send her favorite ornament to the man as token of love. Thus, they are betrothed to each other. In the daytime, the man labors at home and sleeps in the woman's home at night. But early the next morning, he has to return to his home. As they do not live together, most couples love each other dearly and treat each other with impeccable respect. When the woman gives birth to a child, mother or sisters of the man will visit her with generous gifts. Although the father shoulders no responsibility for raising the child, he knows and often goes to see the child. As the entire family consists of just sanguine relatives, family members mostly live in harmony. This peculiar marriage has aroused the interest of both Chinese and foreign scholars studying social formations and marriage customs of matriarchal societies.

A Mosuo woman in splendid ethnic attire.

A Dai village at
Xishuangbanna,
Yunnan.

A Dong Village.

A man of the Derung ethnic group.

A Dongxiang couple.

The ancient city of Lijiang in Yunnan retains its primitive flavor.

Elderly Dongba people of the Naxi ethnic group in Yunnan.

Dongba Script, the world's only remaining hieroglyphs.

Sketch Map of Major Natural and
Cultural Spots in West China

Sketch Map of Mineral and Energy Resources Distribution in West China

Xinjiang Uygur Autonomous Region
Gansu
Inner Mongolia Autonomous Region
Heilongjiang
Jilin
Liaoning
Beijing Munic.
Tianjin Munic.
Hebei
Shanxi
Shandong
Ningxia Hui Autonomous Region
Qinghai
Tibet Autonomous Region
Shaanxi
Henan
Jiangsu
Hubei
Anhui
Shanghai Munic.
Sichuan
Chongqing Munic.
Zhejiang
Guizhou
Hunan
Jiangxi
Fujian
Yunnan
Guangxi Zhuang Autonomous Region
Guangdong
Taiwan
MSAR
HKSAR
Hainan

SOUTH CHINA SEA

South China Sea Is.

Guangxi
Nanning
Guangdong
Guangzhou
Macao
Hong Kong
MSAR
HKSAR
Haikou
Hainan

★ Capital
◎ Provincial or autonomous regional capital
Oilfield with total verified reserves of more than 500 million tons
Natural gas field with total verified reserves of more than 100 billion cubic meters
■ Major coalfield or coal-bearing area
● Copper
Lead and zinc
Copper and nickel
Potash salt
Gold

图书在版编目（CIP）数据

走进西部／黄卫编著；王燕娟译．－北京：外文出版社，2002.9
（中华风物）

ISBN 7-119-03116-3

Ⅰ.走… Ⅱ.①黄…②王… Ⅲ.①西北地区－概况－图集
②西南地区－概况－图集 Ⅳ.K92-64

中国版本图书馆 CIP 数据核字(2002)第 053047 号

"中华风物"编辑委员会

顾　　问：蔡明照　赵常谦　黄友义　刘质彬
主　　编：肖晓明
编　　委：肖晓明　李振国　田　辉　呼宝珉
　　　　　房永明　胡开敏　崔黎丽　兰佩瑾

责任编辑：崔黎丽　李琼芳
图片编辑：李迎迎
摄　　影：兰佩瑾　夏居宪　刘春根
　　　　　孙建平　李　信　房海峰等
英文翻译：王燕娟　沈红梅
英文审定：王燕娟
内文设计：席恒青
封面设计：席恒青

走进西部

黄卫 编著

ⓒ 外文出版社
外文出版社出版
（中国北京百万庄大街 24 号）
邮政编码：100037
外文出版社网址：http://www.flp.com.cn
外文出版社电子邮件地址：info@flp.com.cn
　　　　　　　　　　　　sales@flp.com.cn
外文出版社照排中心制作
天时印刷(深圳)有限公司印刷
中国国际图书贸易总公司发行
（中国北京车公庄西路 35 号）
北京邮政信箱第 399 号　邮政编码　100044
2002 年(24 开)第 1 版
2002 年第 1 版第 1 次印刷
（英）
ISBN 7-119-03116-3/J·1609 （外）
05800 （精）
85-E-547S